AF428270

INDEX

DOLPHINS

Dolphins are masters at identifying who is on their teams and who is not.

Male dolphins make friends or talk to others based on whether that dolphin helped them in the past.

Depending on the sound that the other dolphins make, the dolphin will see whether he likes that dolphin and only then respond to the call. Dolphins judge each other and are mean too !!

A group of researchers flew drones above dolphin groups, recording their behavior through the sounds, tracking their movements underwater and revealing how dolphins respond to the calls of other males.

Dolphins select friends based on past interactions. They reflect on whether the other dolphin has been kind and good to them over the years. If the answer is yes, they initiate interactions. If the answer is no, they actively avoid any form of interaction and try to distance themselves.

SPIDER'S SILK

You will be shocked by the things you did not know about spider's silk.

Did you know that the spiders have limited silk in their body.

Spiders use their silk for 2 major reasons - trapping prey and build a sturdy home.

The silk that spiders produce are stronger than steel and thinner than human hair.

The webs are waterproof and more elastic than any material made by humans.

When the spider needs to move its location or when the web is no longer needed by them, the spider eats the web up. This is because the web contains protein which is a good healthy snack. It is almost equal to eating an insect.

The silk is produced by spiders using the silk glands which is present in their abdomen.

A spider produces 7 different types of silk because they have 7 different silk glands.

Is spider silk used by humans?

string of a fishing rod

String of the violoin

Chinese traditional wear

SQUID EYE

Squids have the largest eyes, But why do they need such large eyes?

One of the most attractive features in all these squids are their eyes which are huge and spherical.

Squids live in the deep trenches of the ocean. That is why it is important for them to have strong eye.

The large eyes increase the surface area of their sight so they can see more. This helps in the detection of predetors.

The eyes of the squid are on the sides. It gives them connection to the optic nerve that is attached to the brain. They can see their entire body at one go.

The squid cannot see color, they can only see black, white and grey. For every different object there is a different shade. The various shades allow them to differentiate between prey and preditor.

The eyes of these squids take up a reasonable amount of space on the squids head. Compared to the human's eye, the squid's eye could be considered about 100 times bigger.

A squid's big eye allows him to detect prey movement in the slightest bit of light,

A squid is good at spotting the bioluminescence of prey found in deeper waters.

Bioluminescent animals are those that produce light is dark places .

DARKNESS AND FASTER CHIRPS

Do crickets chirp faster in the dark ?

Crickets are generally heard better at night when there is hardly any another sound, but many times people confuse this by thinking that the chirps are faster during the night.

The chirps are related to the temperature of the surrounding. In warmer climates the chirps take more time to reach the human ear. Nights are generally colder than the day, thus the sound travels faster. The cricket makes the sound at the same speed but the molecules in the air will make it slower or faster.

Why do they chirp?

This chirping is a mating call to the female crickets. Because they do not have night vision, the cricket relies on sound to detect mates and that is also why their sound is so loud.

The males make this sound by rubbing their wings together. Do all the cricket's chirp sound the same to you? In reality each and every one is different. This helps the females identify the crickets.

SLEEP SNAILS

Have you ever thought about how snails sleep. Do they sleep?

Snails are everywhere - on the land and in the waters. Snails are also hermaphrodites, which means they have both male and female organs.

Snails have an unique sleep cycle, which is very different from yours and mine. Instead of a 24hr cycle, the snails follow a 3 day cycle.

In the three day period the snail will sleep for 13 to 15 hours. They do not wait for the night and sleep whenever they feel tired because they need to do hard work for another 30 hours.

They also sleep to avoid the harsh weathers, where there is no food available. They sleep during the winters (hibernation) and the summers (aestivation). The snails add mucus on their skin so they do not dry up or freeze while sleeping.

NOSY BATS

Did you know that bats use other species private information to hunt them down!

Bats have been using social information to hunt down prey.

They have been doing this for years but humans have only come to know about it lately. Through evolution, bats have developed over hundred hunting strategies.

They use echolocation to navigate. This is where they produce a high pitched sound which will bounce off an object and return to the bats ears.

Bats generally hunt in open spaces which are mainly over waters and above forests.

Bats have an excellent hearing skills.

Most of the bats spend the maximum of their time trying to listen for movements or detect the smell of their prey.

With the help of the echolocation sound that returns, the bats are able to perceive how far the objects are from itself.

Vampire bats reduce their energy usage by simply eavesdropping in the prey's communication.

Thus there are sounds such as the mating call of a frog, the chirping of a bird or insects flapping on wings which the bats think of as dinner calls.

Bats watch others while hunting. They listen for feeding buzzes so they know where the prey is.

SEE THE CHANGE

When it is too dark, mice change the way in which they use their vision.

If the mice are in an extremely dark environment or cannot see clearly, the nerves of their body increase the ability to hear.

The mouse's sensitivity changes to a different frequency and instead of seeing, they listen carefully. Researchers found that there are also changes in the way, that the brain cells interact with each other.

The hearing system of the rat will better when it is dark and allow the rat to hear the smallest of sounds.

During an experiment, researchers examined the brain's activity associated with sound.

They placed a mice in a dark box for weeks and played different tones everyday.

The brains of the mice adjusted to the sounds and associate them with certain ideas or objects. The scientists used to play a specific sound before giving the mouse food. So whenever the sound was made the mice sat - ready to eat.

This new discovery can help in the treatment of visual disease and impairment. It might help scientists cure blindness and visuals aids.

NO CONTROL OF THE EARS

Did you know that your ear move whenever you hear a sounds.

Most animals like dogs, cats and horses have the ability to move their ear (pinna) from the left to right when they hear a sound. Their pinna goes on high alert and twist in directions to identify the place where the sound is coming from.

The human ear makes unconscious and minute movement with the sudden production of sound.

When new sounds are introduced to the human ear, the muscles around that ear become alert and active.

This activity performed by the ear muscles helps them to detect the direction from which the sound is originating. The pinna is considered a vestigial organ, it means a waste organ because humans do not use it for anything. It is just there!

These electrical signals passing caused minute movements of the ear which are invisible to the human eye.

The scientists found that these muscle movement occur when we are exposed to a new sound or we need to focus of someone's voice like the teachers. Sensors were attached to the persons skin which detected movement and change.

The discovery of this muscle can be helpful in treating hearing problems. Hearing aids can be produced in an evolved manner. We can program them to record data too!

BIRD SONGS

Did you know that birds sing to attract females and to mark territory.

Marking territories is the major reason for why the male birds sing. He tries to say "This place is mine, and I am willing to protect it with all my life".

Another reason for the song is the mating call. Male birds have to make sure that their voice is perfect because the female birds are very picky.

The mating season is when the most bird songs are heard. For different birds the mating season and time is different. Most American species of birds also migrate to reproduce.

For species only the male bird sings but there are some exceptions where even the female sings, while some species of birds do not sing at all.

Some birds like vultures and storks make no sound. A crow might 'caw' but these birds do not even make calls and thus never sing.

Scientists also say that these birds songs are therapeutic - so remove those head phones and put away the gadgets. Spotting birds can also make your eye sight better.

HUFF AND A PUFF

The puffer fish have the most unique defect mechanism according to scientists.

The scientific name of a puffer fish is actually Tetraodontid. The species puff up when predators are near. To bloat up in such a manner the pufferfish absorb air and water.

No pufferfish needs to learn how to puff up and they are never taught to do this action. Since the minute they are born, these pufferfish know how to bloat up.

When the puffer fish is frightened or sees a predator, it will open its mouth and widen its jaw. With this open mouth the pufferfish is able to take in 35 gallons in 14 secs.

When the pufferfish is inflated, they can only make very minute movements and lose most of their ability to move. As a result, they only puff up when they realize they won't be able to escape the predator.

The puffer fish will open a closed throat muscle to deflate.

They will slowly release small amounts of water from the mouth. Deflating at one go is dangerous.

Puffer fish have an interesting process where they 'cough' using the muscles of the body which causes the water to go towards the mouth and then slid down the throat into the stomach. The puffer fish grows 3 times more than their usage size.

The hummingbird's main food is sugar, but then why don't they grow fatter?

You will mainly see hummingbirds around flowers because they primary form of nutrition is nectar. This nectar is only sugar, thus you can say that hummingbird eat more sugar than humans do!

The hummingbirds take in vitamins, minerals, protein and carbohydrates to stay healthy. The source of protein for hummingbirds are insects.

A hummingbird is always on the move, and hardly stopping to give itself rest. To always be active, it requires a lot of energy which it gets that from all the sugar they eat.

Hummingbirds will also scavenge insects in flowers, bushes, and trees. Small flies, ants and small spiders are among their favorites. People have spotted hummingbirds eating the soil and scientists think that this is done to get minerals and vitamins.

Along with nectar they eat the pollen too. The hummingbird's diet is extremely wide, so when there is a scarcity of one food item - they can always resort to the other.

If you and I eat the amount of sugar that hummingbirds do, our blood sugar level immediately rises and we become vulnerable to several diseases.

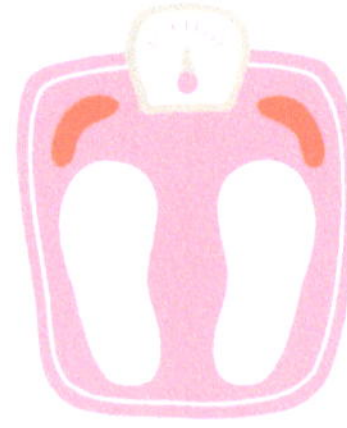

The bird's blood has adapted to digesting sugar. Their heart beats for about 1260 times per minute compared to a humans with is 70 times only !

RATTLE SNAKEZZZZ.

Did you know that rattle snakes sleep at any time of the day.

Snakes do not have moveable eyelids so they do not close their eyes while sleeping. They change their sleep pattern every year.

Because all of the rattlesnake species wait for the prey at one location, they have ample of time while they wait for the food.

The rattlesnakes have spectacles which are clear flaps. The snake can move these eyelids as they wish and thus allows less light to pass through their pupil using these eyelids.

For short intervals of time, the snakes sleeps during the day and night to restore its focus.

Most rattlesnakes have varying choices and prey preferences according to their age and abilities.

Thus when the snakes are waiting at one position for the prey, not all of them take short naps at the same time.

It varies from snake to snake, according to where exactly they are located and how long.

Some species of snakes rest their heads on logs and trees while sleeping. Through this strategic resting position of the head, the snake definitely gets the rest it needs to restore its energy and concentration but it is also open to stimulus so can still hear and sense movement.

SCALY EYES

Learn about how the alligator's eyes is different form all reptiles.

There are 5 MILLION alligators on the earth and they all live in marshy areas.

These animals do not have any other sensory organs so they are dependent on the eyes, which function on land and in water.

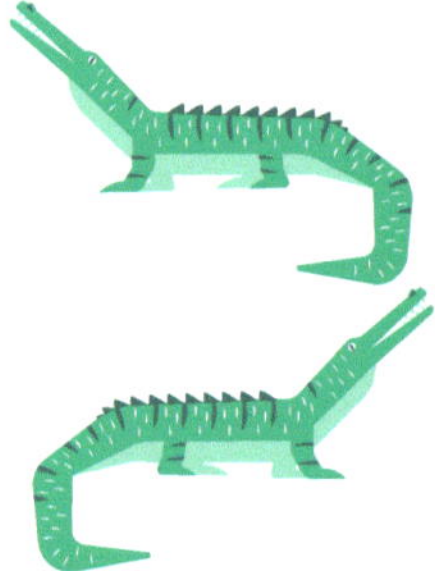

The eyes, nose, and ears of the alligator are all located on the top of its head.

Most of the alligator's body is underwater but its nostrils and eyes are above.

The eyes being at the top allows them to overlook the grass and detect prey.

The eyes of a gator are enormous for his body. They can move in the socket; if attacked, the gator draws his eyeballs back and down into the bony skull, then pushes them back out when the danger has passed.

Their eye's position helps vision in low-light settings like murky water or darkness. Their eyes glow red at night.

A foot of body length is generally equal to 1 inch of distance between a gator's eyes.

The eyes of the gator's face directly to the sides so they cannot see straight in the front.

They cannot see anything directly in front of them, to see these objects the gator would have to completely turn its body - similar to a chicken.

HORSE SLEEP

If someone said that they slept while standing, would you believe them?

Horses have the ability to stand while sleeping. Although, it may seem weird to us, it helps the horse survive.

Earlier, horses lived in open areas and were food for most animals. They had to be alert because they could be attacked at any time.

Whenever a predator showed up the horses needed to run away fast. The standing allows them to be in a position of escape.

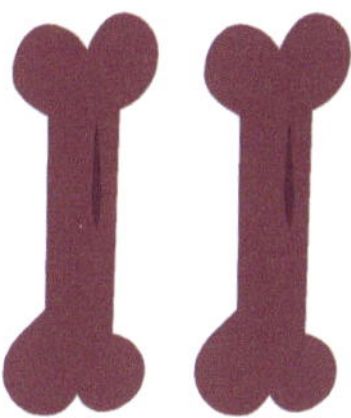

There is an agreement made in the horses muscles and bones. This is where the horse can stand on 3 legs while resting the other one. In this manner they alternatingly give each leg a rest.

Despite the fact that horses can sleep standing up, scientists believe horses need to lie down and sleep once in a while.

Horses can also choose if they want to sleep with their eyes open or closed due to the same reasons as the standing sleep - risk of predators.

Horses have adapted to keeping their eye lids half shut, which means they are half awake. The way they decide to close their eyes all depends of the situation and where they sleep.

ONLY THE J?

The Blue J that appear blue are actually brown !!

They love acorns and live in oak trees.

The Blue J is part of the song bird family, and is native to North America. It is known to be extremely intelligent creatures with complex social systems.

They generally eat berries and smaller fruits but can also eat grains and various kinds of seed such as sunflower seeds etc.

The Blue J's wings have tiny pockets in them that are made of air.

The blue J birds are one of the most attractive species during the season in winter due to their striking color.

Light hits the blue J's air package in the feathers but they do not let the blue light pass like the others.

They are brown in color but they look blue because of the light.

The blue light is absorbed by the birds wing

They make eagle noises to confuse predator's and warn other when a threat is near.

Blue J rub ants of their feathers to remove the acid the ants.

Many hummingbird species have colorful feathers on their throats that have a similar appearance.

Light passing through their feathers is refracted like a prism, creating the impression of rich shades, thanks to the nearly undetectable pockets in their feathers.

The feathers seem significantly duller in colour when viewed in low light or in the dark.

FORTUNETELLER FROGS

Frogs can predict earthquakes better than human machines.

Toads can detect earthquakes days before the ground actually starts shaking.

They use this information to get shelter as soon as possible with enough food storage.

The toads have got this ability through evolution due to the changes that have occured in pond waters.

The scientists studied toads living in a pond near L'Aquila just before a devastating earthquake hit the region.

In the days before the earthquake, the toads began to leave. Slowly from about a 100 toads, zero were left near the pond .

When the rocks under the ground come under pressure due to the earthquake, they release a chemical.

Such particles may ascend to the Earth's surface, affecting things like pond water and the biological materials contained inside it.

The toads react to these chemicals which were released into their ponds and thus find out that a earthquake was coming.

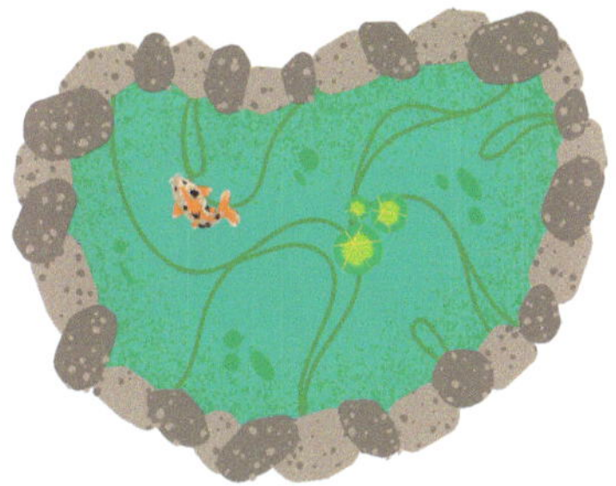

The chemicals also filled the pond with toxins that harm the frogs.

Harmful fungus can actually help kill parasites that attack bees.

There has been a new eruption of a parasite known as 'mite' which affects honey bees.

Although these mites can be killed by chemicals, they have now started to evolve and adjust to almost all climates and make their own adaptations.

Bees are the insects that most of the flowers are dependent on. They help the plants in pollination. Pollination is the first stage of reproduction where the male meets the female. Plants do not have legs, so the cannot move on their own and need external help.

Mites have been troubling the beekeeping industry since decades. Finally hope has come to light when a fungus (M. anisopliae) was discovered that grows through parasites and makes hole in it which kills it.

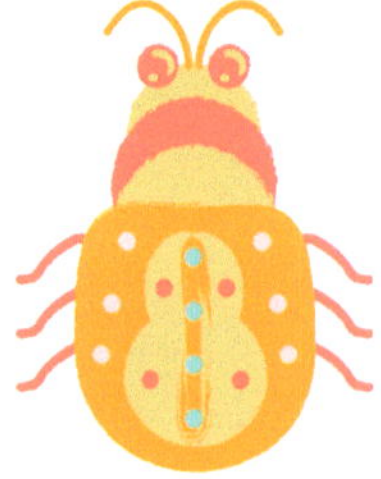

But when they discovered this fungus it was not 100% effective. Scientists first made a strain of the fungus which could survive in all environments and temperatures.

Their next step was to make the fungus more deadlier so they get a guaranteed kill. Since then the fungus has already been used by several farms and is showing a positive result.

DRAGON-BYE

Global warming will kill dragon flies. They will go extinct !

Excessive heat can cause dragonflies to lose their pigmentation or bright colors. It will becomes very hard for them to find a mate as they are no longer attractive without any color.

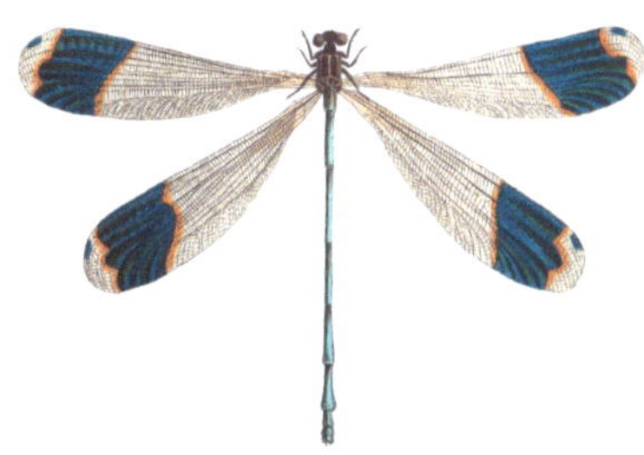

Dragonfly males generally have dark and easily detectable colors on their wings which they use to impress mates and scare away possible rivals.

319 dragonfly species were examined carefully and the scientists compared the same species and dragonfly living in a colder and hotter conditions.

Dragonflies of the same species produced lesser body pigment in hotter conditions compared to the ones in the colder conditions.

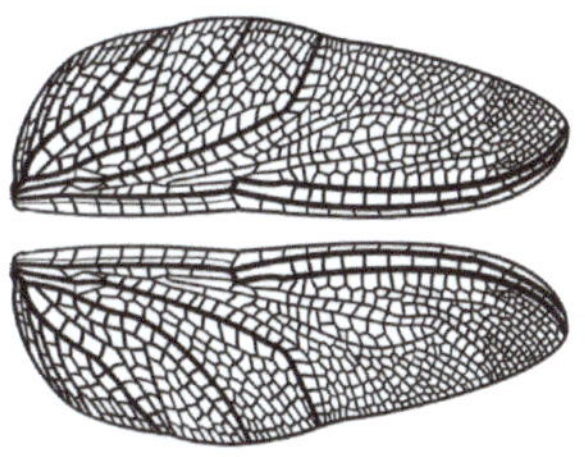

Females are showing no change in wing pigmentation even though they feel the stress from the heat. This causes a concern for the survival of the female dragonfly species when temperatures rise.

Each different species of dragonfly has a unique color combination on their wings. This helps the male and female to identify each other during mating seasons. If males lose their color females will not know who to mate with - no reproduction will occur.

Black feathers around the eagle's eyes makes it look like they are wearing eyeliner.

The black patch around an eagle's eye helps them to ease the process of catching prey.

Eagles are believed to achieve increased concentration and sharper vision through the black patches.

Malar stripe or 'mustache,' are the black patches of feathers under the eyes of the falcon.

The Malar Stripe enables them to reduce sunlight glare and see their prey clearly.

Do you remember somewhere else you have seen these black patches ? On the face for football players ? Yes, football players generally put a streak of black paint under their eys to make sure they can see the fast paced balls and runners.

Scientists who were interested in this phenomenon studied the images of the Peregrine falcons.

The study compared the size, width and height of the malar stripe on 200 birds.

The malar stripes of peregrine falcons were found to be bigger and darker in areas of the world where sunlight is greater.

The scientists still only choose to study the Peregrine falcon. Why you may ask, because they are the most spread species of eagles.

These species are distributed all around the world except Antarctica. Thus giving the scientists an advantage with the natural heat density in one place compared to another.

THE BIG CAT SECRET

Did you know that the tiger's whiskers are secret messengers.

Whiskers aid tigers in discerning their surroundings and navigating through narrow spaces, even in complete darkness.

The whiskers' most crucial function is their ability to transmit information to the tiger's brain.

Just like the fine hairs on our hands and legs that can sense an ant crawling or a chilly breeze passing by, the whiskers on a tiger's chin and face enable them to perceive their surroundings.

Another function of whiskers is that it allows the tiger to understand the distance between two places.

On the end of the tiger's whiskers, there microscopic parts that detects change and sends signals to the brain

This helps them when they need to jump on prey or from rock to rock. The whiskers on the legs help them with the same.

The whiskers contain an organ which acts like an alarm.

The alarms possess remarkable sensitivity, capable of detecting even subtle changes in temperature, wind flow, and scents. When any movement occurs, a signal is swiftly transmitted to the tiger's brain, facilitating their effortless prey detection.

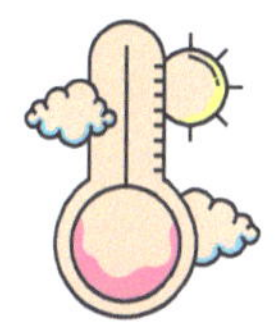

Most animals and even humans have a nervous system that consists of the brain and the nerves in your body.

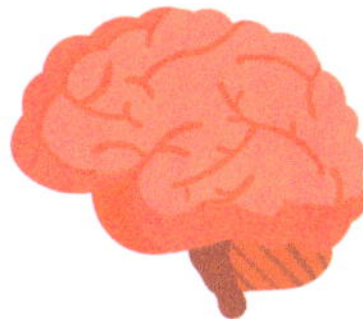

The nerves send messages to your brain whenever there is an action happening so that it aware of what you are doing and can respond.

Killer whales can communicate with other species.

Killer whales can communicate with other species by shifting the sounds that they make according to the type of animal they want to talk to. Until now they have learned the language of the bottlenose dolphins, who they actively socialise with.

A killer whale's natural language is highly intricate, comprising distinct components such as clicks, whistles, and pulsed calls, characterized by bursts of sound with pauses in between.

Due to the close relationship between their sounds, killer whales are capable of imitating dolphin sounds, as both species employ clicks, whistles, and short bursts of sounds.

When killer whales hear the sound of a dolphin click they immediately get excited and playful..

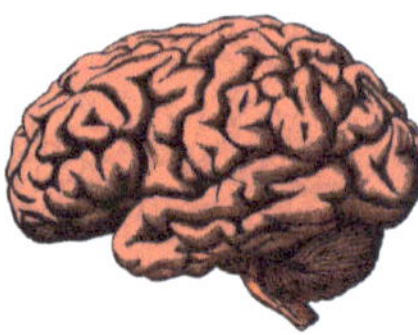

To make the experience better, they understood the pattern of clicks that dolphins make.

This bond also aids in their survival, when it comes to the constant threat of getting entangled in fishing nets. By comprehending the dolphin language, the whales can identify areas of potential danger. If a dolphin emits distress calls, the whales instinctively avoid approaching that specific area.

BATS UPSIDE DOWN

Why do bats sleep upside down.
Is it not uncomfortable ?

Bats hang upside down for many reasons.

Firstly, unlike birds they cannot launch themselves into the air easily because their wings do not have enough strength to propel them forward.

When bats need to fly, they release their grip and fall down - as they start to fall they quickly open their wings .	They could take a running start but their legs are too tiny to make those rapid movements.	Hanging upside down on higher platforms also keeps them safe from predators.

During the day while major predators are out on a hunt the bats are asleep in dark and damp places where their black color easily camouflages.

Not many animals actually have a habit of looking up to check if prey is there and thus saves the bats from getting eaten.

Humans cannot sleep upside down because too much blood will rush into our brains.

The bat's heart, on the other hand, is compact and tiny, allowing it to effectively transmit the little volume of blood even while upside down.

Their claws or talons work in an opposite direction compared to other muscles and their knees also face backwards.

Once their toes and legs are firmly secured, the combination of body weight and gravity allows them to remain suspended. When the leg muscles are flexed, the toes and talons are released.

ROUND AND ROUND

Did you know that marine animals move in a circular manner ?

The megafauna (largest animals) of the sea perform this unique circling motion, where they consecutively move in the water forming a circle at different speeds.

While conducting an experiment to see whether baby turtles can understand direction the scientists found his movement. The turtles were moving in a circle over and over again .

While some argue that circular motion can allow easier swimming, current evidence indicates that the most efficient approach is to swim in a straight line, accounting for factors such as speed, water direction, resistance, and friction.

The circular action proves advantageous for hunting, as numerous studies indicate that these movements are predominantly observed during the animal's hunting periods.

Some male sharks do these circular motions while around females to explain to the female that they are looking for a mate to reproduce with. Turtles use it for navigation.

Circling movements could help to detect the magnetic fields for navigation too just how submarines undergo the same action to obtain their sense of direction.

Why have humans not been able to see this circling movement before?

Because most of these animald hunt at late nights when the entire sea is dark.

HOT OR COLD

Some fish are warm blooded while most of the others are cold blooded.

Despite the ability of cold-blooded fish to regulate their body temperatures in response to the climate, enabling them to survive in various temperature conditions and swim swiftly, they are still not distributed across a wide range of sea temperatures worldwide.

It shows scientists that cold blooded fish such as sharks and tuna are just as vulnerable to the effects of climate change on sea temperature as cold blooded fish.

Being warm-blooded helps them move faster as heat makes the muscles stronger. They can adapt to live in all these different temperatures, they can survive climate change to a extent.

Warm-blooded fishes are competitors over cold-blooded fishes in terms of hunting and migration due to their higher swimming speeds.

These animals do not live in a variety of temperatures even though they have the ability to. Which means that they are at equal risks of climate change compared to any cold blooded species.

FLIGHT EASY

Birds have their unique adaptations for flying or migrating.

Environment and behaviour plays a significant role in a long distance flight adaptations. There are several kinds of flight seen in birds and it all depends on the bird's need.

Understanding the way different organisms vary and in the ways they move and fly can help us also discover conservation techniques to protect them in the future.

The measurement of a bird wing is known as ' hand - wing index' and this measurement helps scientists to find out the length or elongation. This length can also tell us how exactly to bird has adapted to long distance flying.

To make their research successful scientists have studied over 45,801 birds in museums and on the field. This has also helped them understand the special function their wings actually have.

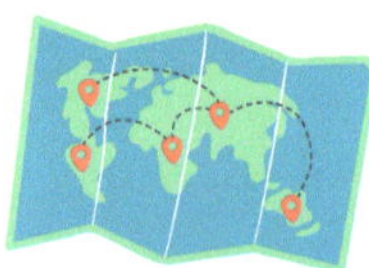

Best-adapted flyers were largely located in high latitudes, whereas stationary birds were mostly found in the tropics.

The scientists discovered that three main variables drive this regional gradient: temperature fluctuation, migration and territory defence.

The reduced geographical ranges observed in tropical species are one example of basic patterns that might be explained by differences in dispersion.

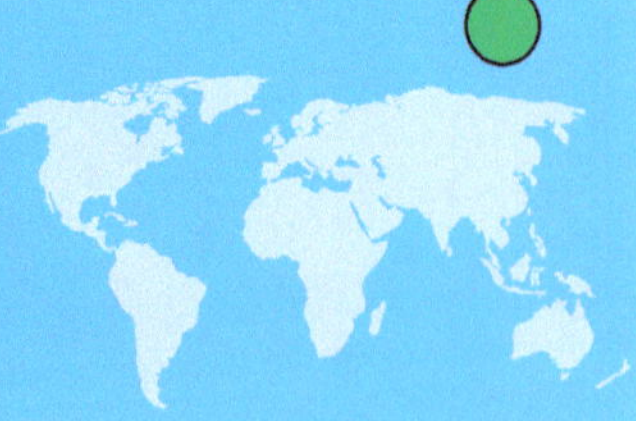

Captive otters have learnt how to juggle stones.

Hunger is the main reason otters juggle stones.

Captive otters or the ones that have been kept in cages are the type of otters that tend to juggle the most and this juggling movement is also known as 'rock juggling'.

Otters tend to juggle very fast and frequently when they are hungry. When they are in cages there is no way for them to get their own food and thus all they can do is wait.

The mammals lay on their backs and throw the stones up into the air. They let the stone land on their body and slide down their neck, then when it has almost reached the end the otters will pick up the stone again and throw it in the air.

Younger otters also tend to juggle more than older otters. Otters are also very good in problem solving and juggle for hunting practice.

Because they are hungry they cannot perform any physical acts and thus revert to simple juggling.

Teeaged and senior otters juggle more than the adults and thus the function and importance of juggling might change as the ages of otters progress.

Juggling is said to help the development of teenager otters and keep the minds of the old ones active.

The reason why otter adults do not juggle is that they are mostly occupied in helping and taking care of their pups.

Did you know that even though jelly fish are so fragile, they still have muscles.

The Bell of the jellyfish is the portion right at the top. It is made up of two components the epidermis and the gastroenteritis.

Their stinging tentacles originate from the bell.

Jellyfish are extremely fascinating because even though 95% of their body is made up of water, they are able to perform complex actions.

They have a ring of muscles at the bottom of their bell which is one of the most important components of the jellyfish's body.

The bell is right at the top of the jellyfish and is open thus fills with water.

The muscles make the bell contract, squeezing the water out and driving the jellyfish ahead, either upward or downward, depending on the location of the bell at the time of compression.

Jellyfish use their muscles to propel themselves forward. When there is a predator near them, they use their muscle to escape faster. But generally, they rely on the water current and just flow with the water.

The string-like structure that comes out from the tentacles of the jellyfish contain stinging cells which are used to injure predators and kill prey.

They have coiled strings which they use to trigger the movement of these string-like structures. It is the most complex mechanism of the jellyfish's body.

COLD SURVIVAL

In japan during the winters, monkeys are seen sitting in rivers and chilling.

Many species of monkeys have adapted to living in extreme cold climates and the temperatures that they can withhold, making them the only non-human primates that can handle this temperature.

They are able to survive in the cold conditions because they have very thick and long fur to secure and save body heat.

This hobby of theirs was discovered in 1963 when a female snow monkey was regularly spotted relaxing in an outdoor hot spring of a hotel. Slowly an increase in the number of monkeys were seen bathing .

EXPERIMENT

Rafaela Takeshita of Kyoto University in Japan and her colleges studies a few female monkeys during the season of winter.

They looked at all aspects of the monkey's life - how much they ate, the amount of time spent in the spring and which of them bathed the most. Even faeces (poop) of the monkey were collected as that should show the researchers the effect of the winter on their internal digestive system.

The superior females spent more time in the water as the fights they engaged in demanded higher energy expenditure compared to the fights of other females. Additionally, monkeys also bathe to relax and maintain hygiene.

WHALE FLUKE

The whale's tail is the most important part of the animal's body.

There are certain features that are similar across all whale species. Among them are flukes. The two lobes of the whale's tail is called flukes. Every whale has a fluke and they slightly differ from species to species.

The two lobes of a whale's tail are separated by a deep cut. Unlike fish, which have vertical tails, whales have horizontal tails. Additionally, flukes in whales lack bones, serving as another distinguishing feature between whales and fish.

The fluke is made up of thick, fibrous connective tissue that are surrounded by a vein network that supplies blood. The flukes are moved up and down by long muscles that run above and below the backbone.

The flukes on a whale's back drive them forward in the water, while the flippers on their sides steer and stops them. They swim with the fluke moving up and down like a paddle, propelling themselves forward with each stroke.

The flukes of whales are also used to take in food. A whale flick-feeds by directing a wave of tiny creatures into his mouth with his fluke. Flick-feeding is similar to kick-feeding in that the whale smacks its prey in order to get it closer to his mouth.

Another function of flukes is to regulate body temperature. The arteries and veins of the flukes may control blood flow to preserve or release heat.

Whales have a very different migration patterns and they even shed their skin.

Because low latitudes are better for whales, the ones that live in the polar regions have started moving there for healthier skin.

This natural phenomena will help humans better preserve these magnificent creatures.

Migrating to warmer water makes it easier for the whales to shed their skin.

It is not only whales but most animals shed their skin, feathers and fur.

Moving to warmer area will help the whales regain their strength and give them the perfect temperature required.

Whales that live in the freezing waters save their body heat by letting the blood flow move away from their skin.

Whales of the freezing Antarctic regions often have no color and they are not in the best moods - they are never happy.

This is mainly because of the horrible skin conditions they have there. The skin of Antarctic killer whales gets different kinds of infections due to bacteria.

But then why do the fish live in the colder region if it is so harmful for them ?

They continue to live there because of the abundance of food.

There are so many available species of fish for the whale to eat.

In normal seas there is a lot of fishing which naturally decreases the amount of fish present there.

ITCHY BITES

Why do Mosquito bites itch so much ?
Is there a chemical they use ?

Did you know that the mosquitoes find us by following the trail of carbon dioxide we breathe out ?

They start to smell our skin and identify whether there are any chemicals on it or not.

Only female mosquitoes suck human blood.

When female mosquitoes are pregnant they have human blood to get more protien and energy.

When a mosquito lands on your arm or legs, she will first push the sharp needle like mouth into the human skin.

The mosquito put their saliva, 'mozzie spit' into the human skin.

The Mozzie spit also causes the red and itchy bumps on our skin known as mosquito bites. Those "itchy bites" are our body's reactions to mozzie spit.

We all respond differently to mosquito bites, just as we all react differently to chemicals, or environmental allergies.

While some people experience immense, swollen masses that cause discomfort, others may only have a small red area on their skin.

Applying a cream to bites that are swollen or itching is the best method to relieve them (this will help reduce swelling).

Applying an anti-itch cream may also be beneficial. Importantly, try not to scratch too much since as soon as you break the skin's surface, you risk secondary infection, and that painful lump will rapidly grow into a scabbing.

It is important not to scratch the skin when you have a mosquito bite because it swells up even more and the mozzie spit can then cause harm to the body.

All sea birds have longer beaks, but why do puffins not ?

Sea birds that have large beaks are able to make longer flights.

The beak causes 10% to 18 % of the body temperature change even though it takes up only 6% of the body's surface area.

The large beaks of the Tufted puffins help them to maintain and regulate body temperatures which is change that helps them to fly for longer periods.

The beak has an association to the energy used when the birds are flying.

Flying takes up a major chunk of the bird's energy. There is an energy expenditure of 31 times greater than when they rest.

The usage of such large amounts of energy produces large amounts of heat and thus most birds have evolved to have a larger beak which helps them to cool down.

A puffin - like bird known as the thick-billed murres produces as much heat as the light bulb while flying.

The body temperature regulation has played a role in influencing the beaks of the puffins.

Researchers tried to understand if the puffins used their beaks to let the excessive heat escape.

Because a bird's body is insulated due to its feathers, it cannot regulate its temperature by respiration.

Instead, when the bill needs to cool down, it acts as a radiator, similar to how humans sweat on a hot day.

No one can escape boredom and it occurs in everyone's life.

Boredom is the state of feeling disinterested in one's surroundings, having nothing to do or feeling that life is dull.

Scientists found that the major problem astronaut's travelling to mars would face is not the toxic air, lack of food or a crash landing - But is truly **Boredom.**

They predicted that the boredom would cause the astronauts to experiment with the spacecraft which could damage the equipment. The astronauts are likely not to do their job correctly because they grow tired of doing the same thing again.

Boredom is most common disorder, where they find it hard to concentrate. People who find it hard to express themselves are isolated and alone.

Although boredom can waste your time, It has certain benefits.

Younger people feel more bored compared the elders. This is because there is a part in our brain that is used in self control and controlling the boredom. But this organ fully develops only in the starting on adult hood.

Research shows that boredom increases creativity. It inspires people and gives them more time to reflect of themselves.

BRAIN FREEZE

Have you ever drank a cold beverage and then felt a painful sensation in your brain?

A brain freeze is a brief and intense sensation of pain felt near the forehead. It occurs when you consume something cold quickly.

We might feel the pain in our brains, but the freeze is taking place in the mouth itself!!

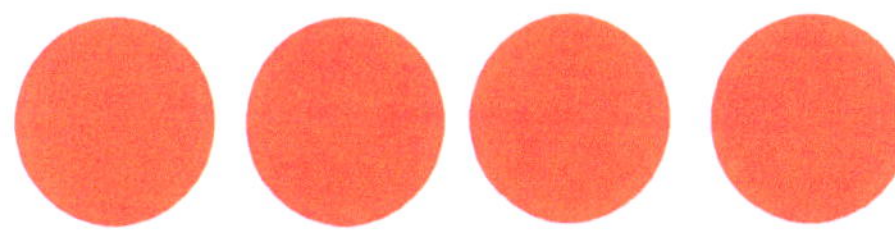

There is a network of blood vessels right below your skin that provide blood to the brain and the face.

When a cold substance enters, the temperature of the mouth suddenly drops and blood vessels shrink. Now blood will not be able to flow to the brain.

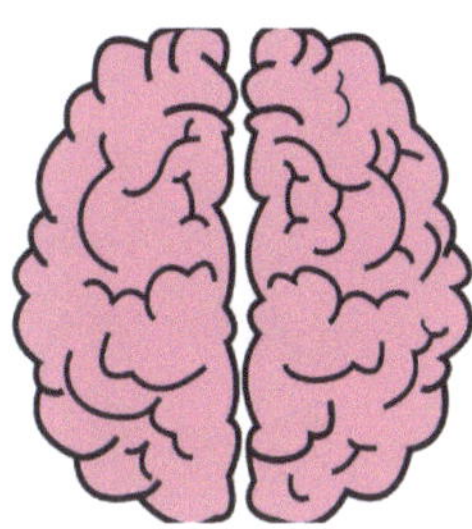

With lesser oxygen and blood traveling to the brain, the head will start to hurt, giving you a signal that it needs the oxygen. The human brain cannot function without oxygen and blood.

MASTER MIND

Have you wondered how your arm knows when and how to pick up the phone ?

A human brain contains 86 billion nerve cells which are called neurons. Using chemicals and electrical signals the neurons can communicate with each other. They are the building block of the brain.

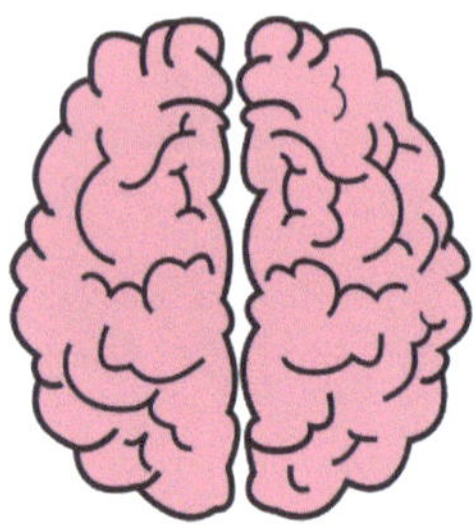

The information travels from the tip of the neuron all the way to the end, where it synapses (the information will get passed on to the next neuron present.

There are about a million pieces of information passing through your brain currently.

The information is sent all the way up to the brain. The brain will then decide what to do and how to react.

Once the brain has decided the reaction, it will send a message to the glands and muscles of the body and tell them what to do.

The brain is also in charge of the way we remember things and how our experiences change our personality. There are nerve cell endings present in a human's ear, mouth and nose. These sensory organs will detect sounds and will directly announce it to the brain.

The billions of neurons working together also help determine emotions and ways in which an individual feels.

THIN TRICK

Do you have friends that can go on eating but never put on weight ?

A research team has found a gene that is present in very few lucky people on this planet that does not allow them to get fatter.

First this was just considered a natural phenomenon but now scientists have discovered that the reason is genetics.

2.8 million people die every year from obesity. Obesity can also cause an increase in blood pressure, diabetes, heart disease symptoms and COVID - 19.

There are common genetic variants that are connected to the appetite which makes it more likely for an individual to put on weight.

There is a group of 50 genes working together to prevent an increase in weight. The proteins that lower your body mass are present in the brain.

Genes are the basis for the signals and responses that guide food intake, and small changes in these genes can affect their levels of activity.

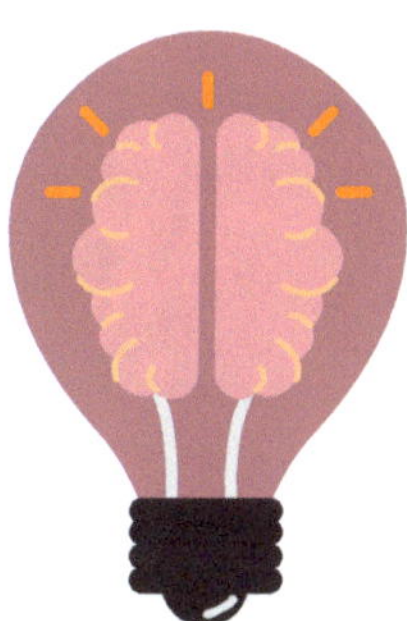

The fat tissue in our body sends signals to the brain which then controls how much food we eat. The brain combines these signals sent with information from the body.

SHARK = MAN

Did you know that human teeth are as strong as shark teeth ?

Human teeth might not look like the ones of sharks but are equally strong.

Human's teeth muscle is softer because it is made up of minerals that are also found in bones.

To confirm this theory scientists broke shark and human teeth into micro - pieces and found that they look the same.

The only difference a shark tooth has from a human's will definitely be the shape, size and number but sharks also have a muscle coating on their teeth.

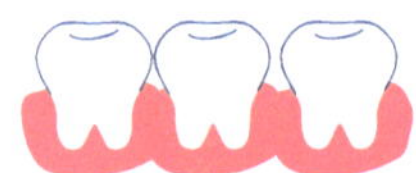

Human teeth have crystals which are bound together with a colony of muscles and are filled with protein to prevent teeth from cracking.

The total strength of human teeth, was found to be comparable to that of shark teeth due to their structure, according to the researchers.

To determine how hard the teeth of the shortfin shark and tiger shark were, they examined every element of the fluorapatite crystals.

X-ray diffraction method = technique used in materials science to determine the crystallographic structure of a material.

Scanning electron microscopy = this is a scanning method of the type of electron microscope that produces images of a sample by scanning the surface with a focused beam of electrons.

Did you know that babies hardly blink.

Adults blink up to 15 times a minute, a baby's frequency for blinking can be as rare as one blink per minute, with the average of 2 - 3 times per minute.

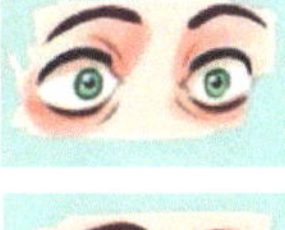

This information can help scientists determine the functioning of the baby's brain because blinking is associated with neurotransmitters.

The neurotransmitter is called dopamine and it can alter blinking levels.

Some diseases increase or decrease dopamine level. This causes excessive blinking or lack of blinking.

Blinking helps us protect ourselves and the eyes from an external object are going to hit it.

If you see a fast moving object coming our way, the first instinct of humans is to close their eyes. We continuously blink, to keep our eyes wet, not allowing them to dry up.

Babies have just been exposed to vision for the first time. Thus they have to work hard to get adjusted and familiarize themselves with all these now objects.

It could be a natural phenomenon to get the babies extra time to take in all the aspects of their world.

As stated above the blinking process of your body is directly connected to dopamine.

During the early stages of development, when babies are still growing, their dopamine system is not fully mature. The body regulates the utilization of existing dopamine at a slower rate, allowing the development of other crucial body parts.

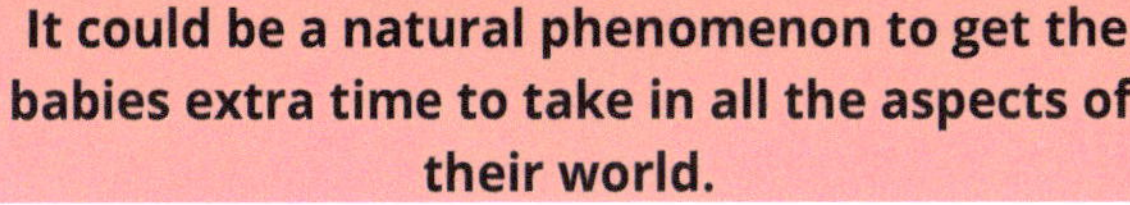

PINKY PROMISE

No other finger can survive without the pinky.

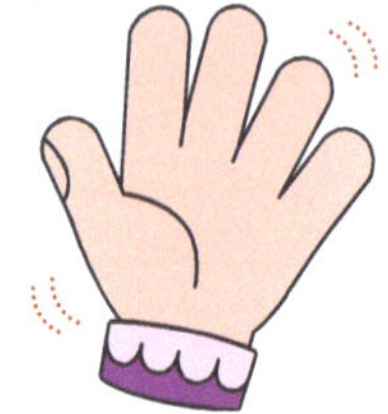

our pinky finger compromises about 50% of our hand's strength. Your index, thumb and middle fingers are for pinching, grabbing, holding - the pinky works with the ring finger to provide power.

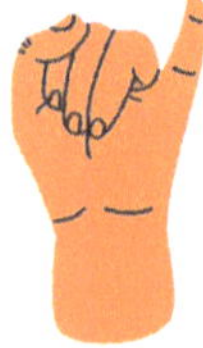

Without a fully functioning pinky, you will be unable to move fingers voluntarily and need to deliberately assist them, the fingers are unable to bend too! Due to this, doing day to day tasks such as writing, holding a glass of water or even having a bath can become cumbersome,

Injuring the pinky is far worse than impairing the other fingers. An injury to the index finger will only affect that finger, but a problem in the pinky it affects all the fingers.

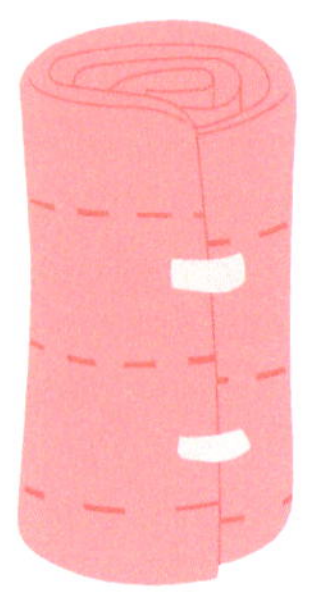

Finger fractures are very common and almost all of them occur on the pinky itself, this is because the pinky is all along the edge and has no protection

Try this - put all your fingers down one by one starting from the thumb all the way to the pinky. Notice that when you lower the first four fingers only they move while the others are intact. But when you move the pinky, you involuntarily move the ring and the middle finger.

Even the recovery and treatments to pink injuries are and should be taken very seriously. Some of the existing curing methods include Heat, ultrasound, neuromuscular stimulation, splinting, and manual rehabilitation.

GOOD NIGHT

A human on average sleeps for about 25 years!! but why?

Sleep is determined by a reduction in the awareness we have about our environment and low levels of physical activity. Sleep also consists of circadian rhymes. The circadian rhythm is a pattern of your mental, physical and behavioral self that follows the 24 hour day cycle.

The sleep - wake cycle in our body is programmed by different parts of the brain working together. These parts of the brain mainly include the hypothalamus, thalamus and pons.

Sleep is also controlled by hormones (messengers) in the body. These hormones are present in different parts of your body which will release them at the perfect time.

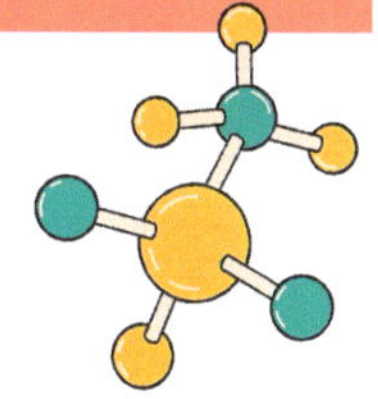

Sleep is needed to restore all the resources we have used up during the day.

Just like when bears hibernate when there is no food, human sleep when they do not have enough energy.

If we are awake 24/7 there will be no way for the body to get those materials again and at one point we would run out of all those essential resources we need.

In the ancient times, sleeping would prevent people from getting eaten by predator's. Because most predators used to hunt at night, humans got an advantage because they were sleeping. This did not draw attention.

THIRST HUNT

Water is the reason you are surviving !!

Water is essential for everyday life- to keep our body running, more than 70% of your body is water.

Our need for water is vital to your survival. It helps with the digestion of food along with aiding certain functions in the body to take place.

You have probably felt thirst before a nagging ache in the back of your throat, a distracting temptation to put down whatever you're doing and go get something to drink.

When there is a lack of water in our body there are a number of changes that our body undergoes . The blood changes and adjusts to the body temperature.

The minerals, vitamins, and nutrients in the body remains constant, while it is the decrease in water level that leads to an increase in their concentration.

A special part on the brain known as the lamina terminalis is responsible for making us feel thirsty.

The brain cells in this area have the ability to sense the changes the body is making and know if you have lesser amounts of water that actually needed. This organ is located towards the front of the brain.

The lamina terminalis, being located outside the blood-brain barrier, can communicate with other parts of the body, so it can assess the water levels.

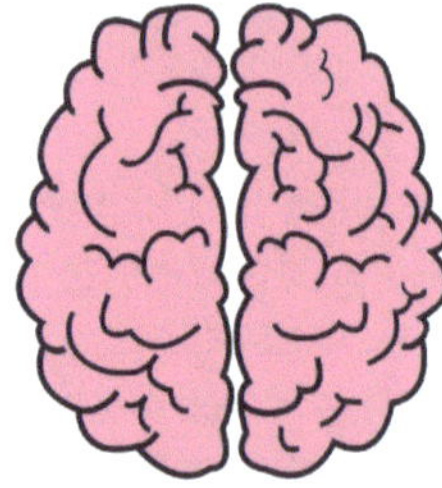

So when these other parts detect any activity that relates to the lack of water they immediately pass it onto the lamina terminalis.

GUT FEELING

Have you ever had that feeling which tells you to do something even though it is dangerous?

The gut feeling also considered our sixth sense, is an insight into our deep internal feeling through which comes the faith.

There is a saying 'trust your gut' it tells you to trust that intuition that is always true to yourself.

It is an intuition that helps us make decisions, it is just like a voice telling you what could be right or wrong when there is an ambiguous situation put in front of you.

Scientists suggest that even personal inclinations towards certain actions or directions can be beneficial.

These gut feelings undoubtedly hold significance for the body and assist in making correct decisions.

Most people describe it as a small voice that you often 'hear' telling them what to do and what is the right path to take.

A gut feeling evokes several sensations and emotions at one time and thus it becomes hard to keep track of all of them.

Along with all the physical signals, one can also develop anxiety and an ecstatic feeling in positive situations.

Although we call them gut - feeling, they do not originate in your gut at all ! They mostly come from the brain. This is where the name 'gut feeling' has originally come from because we feel all the effects of these emotions in the stomach area.

SOCIOCULTURE

Did you know the society can change the way you act without you even knowing it.

The sociocultural theory focuses on the effect that society has on an individuals growth and development. This Is stressed in the interaction between people and the cultures around them.

The sociocultural theory was proposed by Lev Vygotsky. He also thinks that society is responsible for a child's higher - order thinking capacity. According to him, the key aspect for learning a new concept has to be on the bases of interaction.

The Zone of proximal development is one of the most important parts of sociocultural theory.

The Zone of Proximal Development is the area between what a learner can do on their own and what they can do with adult direction or in partnership with more capable classmates.

This zone consists of all the skills, attributes, attitudes, concepts and knowledge a child cannot understand by themselves but are able to master with the guidance of someone known.

This entire theory has also helped teachers understand the importance of play in learning. The children can enjoy what they are doing and learn better due to that happy feeling.

He stated that through playing the children are able to extend their intellectual abilities to a great length and enhance the understanding of the world in the children.

YAWN

If you stop yawning, you can get extremely sick.

Did you know that just thinking of yawning can make you do it?

It happens to everyone including animals. Doctors suggest that you should not ever stop yourself from yawning because it is essential to the body.

Yawning allows more oxygen to reach your brain. We yawn to regulate or adjust our temperatures in the brain.

If your brain gets overheated, yawning helps the body cool the brain down so that it keeps functioning.

Another common reason for why we yawn includes tiredness. When your brain starts to slow down it causes your temperature to drop.

Because your brain is unable to work effectively, your body tries to provide it with more oxygen so that it gets a boost.

But then why do you yawn in the morning, even though you are not tired?

Yawning gives your body a waking call. When you yawn it stretches out your muscles and allows the body to stretch its joints and ligaments. It also forces blood all the way up to your face, which brings the brain to alert mode.

It is often seen that if a person in the same room as you yawns, you are likely to yawn too. Sometimes even watching a video or listening to an audio that involved yawning, can make you yawn.

BLIND DREAMS

Have you ever wondered how the blind can see dreams ?

An individual who is blind does have dreams but they do not see images. Their dreams could include everything from their other senses - just like smell, sounds, they could feel the taste of certain food and touch.

The dreams could maybe be about past memories or experiences or it could build on what they have experienced in the day.

For example, a person who has color blindness isn't suddenly going to start seeing colors in their dreams, but they will see normal object and images in black and white.

A person who was not blind from birth and had the ability to see before will experience entirely normal dreams, which will often revolve around their past memories.

Charles Bonnet syndrome enables individuals to perceive light and flashes of color, and these same aspects are often reflected in their dreams.

People who are legally blind might be able to perceive light in a non - visual way. This started off with an experiment with mice done by a Harvard graduate student. They bred mice who were blind and saw that they could still detect light

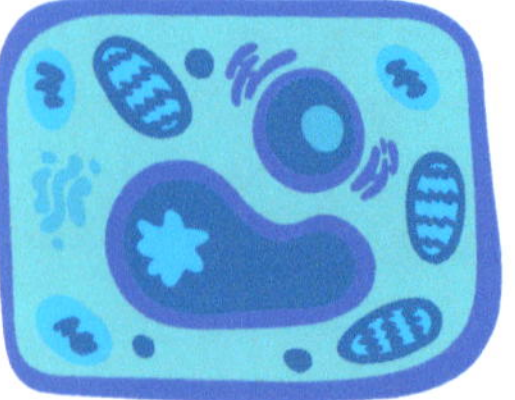

They found special cell on the nerve that connects the last layer of your eye to the brain. These cells have the ability to detect light but not objects.

METABOLISM

How do processes in your body take place, who gives the organs instructions?

Metabolism is a reaction that breaks down any type of food into energy. This energy that our body produces is used to walk, run, talk and do daily activities. There are proteins in the body that control metabolism.

Did you know that there are thousands of metabolic reactions happening at the same time and all of them are controlling your body - trying to keep you healthy and make you stronger.

When the digestive system in our body is at work, it converts the protein into amino acids, breaks down the fat into fatty acids and converts the carbohydrates into glucose. The body then uses these products to provide energy for itself. They are absorbed by blood that transfers them into the other cells.

When they have finally reached the cell, there are enzymes present that speed up the process of 'mobilizing'.

Through the process of mobilizing energy is released and used by the body or the excess is stored in the tissues such as the muscle, liver and fat of the body.

The anabolic processes are those that build up tissues and energy. They are used in the formation of cells and stroage of energy. Smaller molecules turn into complex ones.

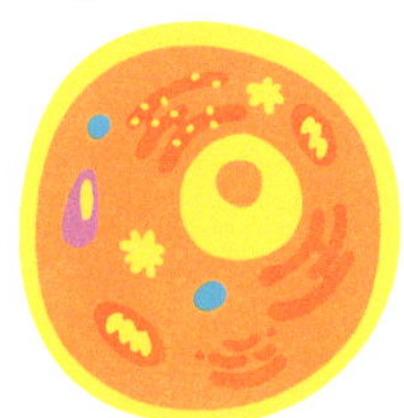

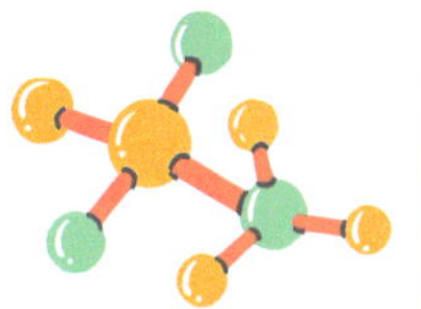

The catabolic process break down larger molecules into small ones. For example, They break down energy storage when your body is doing any physical activity.

THE FIGHT

The immune system fights all the germs in your body, they are the knights of the body.

Every human being has an immune system in their body which is responsible for fighting against infectious germs. The immune system attaches to the germs that enter our body and kill them.

Due to its crucial role in long-term health, the immune system operates in partnership with two other systems.

It consists of primary WBC's (white blood cells) which fight against the diseases. Under the White blood cells there are different kinds - phagocytes and lymphocytes.

The phagocytes help in chewing living organisms whereas the lymphocytes help the body to kill viruses.

There are two types of lymphocytes: B lymphocytes and T lymphocytes. Initially, they both originate in the bone marrow. B lymphocytes serve as the body's intelligence system, identifying targets and guiding defenses towards them. T cells, on the other hand, function as the troops, responsible for eliminating intruders detected by the intelligence system.

When a human recognises an unknown substance entering the body, the immune system starts working immediately.

Acquired immunity - a form of immunity that arises when an individual's immune system reacts to a foreign substance or microorganism, for instance, following an infection or vaccination.

When you observe your fingers while swimming, don't they look like an old man's hand?

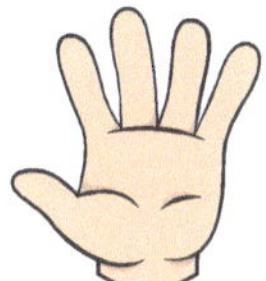

Wrinkles form on your fingers, if you stay in the water for more than 5 minutes. In hot water wrinkling can take place on your hands, feet and skin in about 3.5 minutes.

The skin itself allows the water to pass through the first few layers. The entire wrinkling process is related to the human nervous system.

The nervous system is a group or network of nerves and their function is to send the brain's messages to the different parts of the body.

We also know that wrinkling is linked to the shrinking of blood vessels. The small pipes that transport blood across your body are known as blood vessels.

Do you think you will be able to pick up that object easily while your hands are all wet ?

These wrinkles, scientists believe, are formed by the body to allow your grip to become better during wet situations. The wrinkles on our toes help us walk across the surface safely and avoid slipping.

If wrinkly fingers are good for us, why aren't our fingers always wrinkled?

If you have noticed, when your fingers are wrinkled they become very soft and the skin starts to peel.

In water, this is not a problem as it is very smooth but when exposed to the air on land, there are several particles that could cut the skin.

You could also get the trench feet syndrome, which is where your feet grow completely white and massive amounts peel off.

HUMAN < FISH

Humans' attention span is so less that even goldfish can focus more than us.

The average attention span of a human is only 8 seconds. And the most shocking part is that it is even lesser than a goldfish's attention which lasts from about 9 seconds.

Given various objects and inventions in our modern society, it is easy for humans to identify numerous distractions in their rooms alone, potentially reaching a hundred or more items.

In the year 2000, the average attention span was 12 secs and now it is as less as 8 secs only. Can you imagine that even a simple fish can concentrate more than us.

This information was gathered from a study dating back to 2015 in Canada. Where 2,000 people were surveyed and the brain activity of about 112 people was measured while they did several different tasks.

According to these researchers, our attention is also influenced by the task at hand. When we are driving a car, our attention span is high due to the life-or-death nature of the situation. However, if we are asked to put clothes in the laundry, we might simply walk up and toss them in without much thought or focus.

The attention span also varies from person to person. If you read this enitre page without any distraction - you are part of the focused group !!

SUN'S DARKENING

Have you ever noticed that your skin color darkens after spending a day at the beach?

In the summers everyone almost lives on beaches and in pools, cooling off the hot summer climate. Have you noticed that when you come out of the swimming pool, you see that the color of your skin has slightly changed. This change of color is known as tanning.

The sun contains two types of ultraviolet radiation that can affect your skin. Ultraviolet radiation are harmful light waves produced by the sun that changes your skin tone.

The types of ultraviolet rays are UVA and UVB.

UVB rays are the worst ones and cause the upper layers of skin to burn when it is in contact with the sun for too long, this causes a sunburn.

The UVA waves go deep down into our skin and react with the lower layers of skin. The is reaction happens in the cells of the body called **melanocytes.**

The products of this reaction is melanin which is a dark brown pigment and this pigment is what makes our skin look darker. Melanin is the body's defence against skin blistering.

It effects the blood vessels and nerves around that area and can have negative effects on the immune system - making it harder for the body to fight certain diseases of the skin.

All of us have seen the wrinkles on the faces of senior citizens and we think it is because of their age. But it is truly because of their exposure to the sun. They have been spent so many years outdoors !

DEJA VU

It is the feeling of having already experienced the present situation.

Have you ever visited a country and had a strong feeling that you have been here before even though you have not ?

You are experiencing deja vu! This is just a strong gut feeling that rises in the body but what you feel is rarely true in reality.

70% of the world's population have experienced this phenomena at least once in their lives. The sensation generally involves most of the senses - sight, sound, smell, taste and touch ; and thus they feel extremely real.

This term was coined in 1876, by a French scientist.

Different scientists have their own conceptions of the definition of deja vu, but universally it is recognised as "the feeling that you've seen or experienced something before when you know you haven't."

Associative deja vu

This is the most common type of deja vu that occurs to healthy and normal individuals. You generally see, smell or hear or experience a situation that builds a strong feeling in the gut, telling you that this has happened to you before.

Biological deja vu

Individuals with other disorders and diseases often experience this Deja vu. There are certain regions of the brain where the déjà vu signals originate.

SICKLED CELL

The disease that changes the shape of your blood.

The sickle cell disease is where the RBC's (red blood cells) are not in the correct shape and thus oxygen cannot be transported effectively.

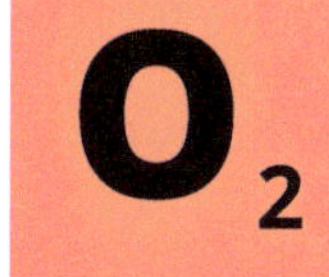

Red blood cells usually have a disc-like structure with a hollow section in the middle, but in this disease they grow to be the shape of a crescent moon.

The shape is the a disadvantage because while moving, they can get stuck with the other cells.

The Cresent shape causes a clot to flow which leads to a blockage of blood vessels that are important to the heart. This disease directly can cause death but generally causes pain and organ damage.

SYMPTOMS

People feel their entire body aching, when their blood flow stops and they do not get as much energy as needed.

The disease can also be triggered by cold, illness and dehydration.

Most of the pain generally lasts for a few hours or days, so it can be treated at home. But the severe ones need to be addressed in the hospitals.

CAUSES

Sickle cell disease occurs when a person inherits two sickle cell genes, one from each parent. If your parents have the disease, it is possible for you to get it. A problem with the haemoglobin (pigment in the blood) can trigger the diesease.

THE EARS

How can you understand which sound is coming from where?

Have you heard thunder ?

Have you heard your own voice ?

Have you heard a cars honk?

I am guessing yes ! because we all have ears and these parts of our body are what we use to hear.

There are two components of the ear that work together and send the information to the brain as a final step - The outer ear and the inner ear.

Outer Ear

The outer ear is made up of the pina. This is known as an external organ because it is outside the body.

In humans the pinna is also called a 'vestigial organ ' which means a waste organ because there is no use of the pina.

The outer ear is also made up of cartilage which is a flexible material. Wax present helps to trap dust.

Unlike animals that can move their pinna automatically when they hear noise, we humans cannot do that.

Inner Ear

The vibrations that are present in the middle ear turn into nerve signals when they reach the inner ear.

The cochlea and the semicircular canals are the two main parts of the inner ear.

The semicircular canals are three tubes. The canals are filled with fluid and have hair inside, their primary function is to help you balance.

The cochlear nerve is attached to the cochlea and sends information of the sound you hear to the brain.

PARKINSONS

The most severe brain disorder! that causes excessive shaking.

Parkinson's disease damages your central nervous system, this includes your brain and the spinal cord.

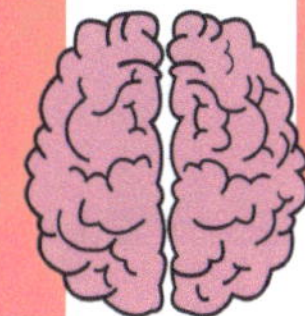

The central nervous system controls all the movements done by the human body.

THERE IS NO CURE FOR THIS DISEASE.

The most common symptom is the constant trembling of the hand, their hands are always shaking. They cannot do any action that involves the hands such as writing, picking up an object etc.

The patients also have trouble remaining balanced, impairment is walking, stiffness and general slowness in performing everyday activities.

Because of their trouble with balance and walking, the people with parkinsons tend to fall down alot and this results in broken bones.

Due to their constant pain and suffering, they can become susceptible to depression. Their existence is characterized by pain, which increases day by day.

There is a collection of cells in the inner sections of your brain known as the basal ganglia.

This group of neurons is responsible for motor movements and controls every action we do.

A person that has Parkinsons, will have certain damage that has occurred in these cells.

These nerve cells make a substance known as dopamine and it is a hormone - a messenger.

This hormone is sent to other parts of the brain and tells the body to perform certain movements.

The mouth helps in self expression, speaking and even posture!.

Our mouth and teeth are used every time we smile, frown, converse, or eat.

Our mouths and teeth allow us to create various facial expressions, form words, eat, drink, and start the digestive process.

Some noises are generated by the tongue striking the teeth or the roof of the mouth.

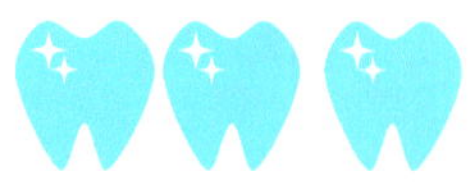

Our teeth rip, cut, and grind food in preparation for swallowing when we eat.

Teeth, with the lips and tongue, aid in the formation of words by controlling airflow out of the mouth.

The roof is also known as the Palate. Its front part is mostly made of bones and thus called the Hard Palate.

This hard palate segregates the mouth and the nose.

After the hard palate comes the soft palate, it is a division between the throat and the mouth.

The moment we put something in our mouths, the soft palate closes the passages to the nose from the throat so no food can enter.

The top of the tongue is known as the papillae - the side with the tiny bumps.

These bumps are actually our taste buds. Four main kinds of taste buds are found on the tongue.

While we are chewing our salivary glands come into activation and start to produce saliva(spit).

Saliva helps to moisten the food and break it down. It becomes easier to chew, swallow and digest food in the present of saliva.

Sounds you make can cause damage to the heart.

Many sounds produced in the environment mainly by humans are unwanted and unnecessary.

They cause harm to different aspects of a human's mind and body but have the worst impact on the heart.

Loud noise may disrupt sleep, evoke rage, and induce diseases which are caused by a reduction in blood supply to the organ.

Encountering extremely loud noises regardless of pitch or tone can cause impairment in a child's memory and learning system.

There is an 8% increase in getting any form of heart disease if you are exposed to uncomfortably loud noises.

People who work in a factory have many heart and blood flow problems. They hear sounds from 90 - 100 decibels everyday which damages their inner ear which causes hearing loss.

If there is a constant loud noise playing for at least 1 hour, it causes high blood pressure, increase in heart rate and an increase in hormone stress level.

Scientists also learn that only 1 exposure to an airplane sound at night or train noise can ruin your entire sleep quality.

When a loud noise is heard it automatically alerts the body's limbic system, that is concerned with the body's emotional situation. When a sound is heard the limbic system releases stress hormones which lead to inflammation in the body.

4 OF TEETH

The number 4 is apparently the favorite number of our teeth.

The number 4 is the favorite of your teeth, because just like we have 4 different types of teeth, each tooth is made up of 4 tissues.

Humans have the ability to develop two sets of teeth.

The first set is developed after birth and are called the milk teeth. These baby teeth start to fall off from the age of 6.

New teeth start growing instead of them. We eventually get a 32 tooth set of permanent teeth.

DIFFERENT TISSUES

The first is the pulp which is the innermost section of the tooth. It contains different tissues, nerves and cells.

The pulp is divided into two parts: the pulp chamber in the crown and the root canal in the root of the tooth.

Blood vessels and nerves enter the root through a tiny hole and extend into the pulp chamber via the canal.

The pulp is surrounded by dentine. It is a hard yellow material that makes up the majority of the tooth and is as tough as bone.

Enamel, the body's toughest tissue, covers the dentine and forms the crown's outermost layer.

It protects teeth from dangerous germs and temperature fluctuations from hot and cold meals by allowing them to endure the pressure of chewing.

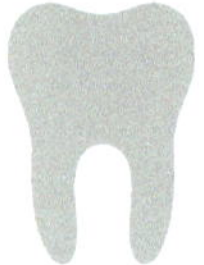

The next is the layer of Centinum, its primary function is to hold the tooth in place with the jaw.

BRAIN BASICS

Do you remember what you ate yesterday? Why do u feel sad and happy?

There are 4 primary components of the brain that are the most important- Cerebrum, Cerebellum, Brain stem, and Hypothalamus.

THE CEREBRUM

The cerebrum is the biggest structure in the brain and it helps in THINKING.

The cerebrum is the storage of your memory. It helps you remember both short term and long term events.

It controls voluntary muscle movement and helps you choose or make a decision.

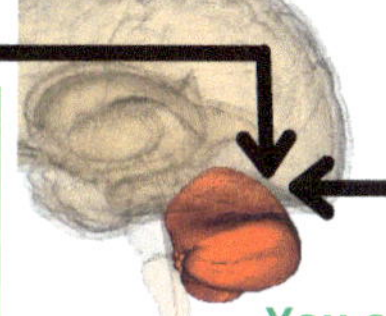

It is responsible for knowing how to play your video games, how to solve a problem, how to dance and act. .

THE CEREBELLUM

This part is all the way at the back of your brain and is just below the cerebrum.

This organ of the brain is vital as it handles balance, movement and coordination.

You can get up and move about, thanks to your cerebellum.

THE BRAINSTEM

The brainstem is in charge of all the simple functions that keep us alive. This includes - breathing, blood flow and digestion.

It is located below the cerebrum and ahead of the cerebellum.

It is very important as it connects the entire brain to the spinal cord.

THE HYPOTHALAMUS

The hypothalamus is the body's temperature regulating center. The hypothalamus always knows what the body temperature is and does its best at delegating tasks.

CEREBRAL PALSY

It is a brain disease that affects the way you walk !!

Cerebral palsy (CP) is a brain disorder that is one of the most dangerous. CP directly affects the brain and your body does not have any source of control or information regulation.

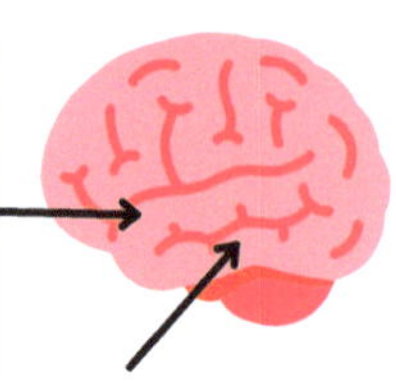

It affects muscle coordination and body movements. People with this disease have a lot of trouble controlling their movements or generating the movements on their own.

THE 3 TYPES

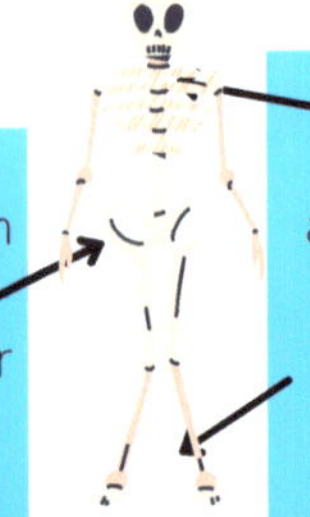

SPASTIC
This is a most common form of CP. Individuals do not have the ability to relax their muscles and the muscles are always stiff.

ATHETOID
This form of CP directly affects your ability to move. All of a sudden a person's legs might start kicking or their hands might start shaking vigorously.

ATAXIC
this primary includes the problems with balance and coordination. All their movements are shaky and they can never stay straight.

Cp develops in babies who are premature and are underweight. Babies who do not get sufficient amounts of oxygen also are vulnerable to this disease.

And this disease develops when the baby is in the womb itself or during the first few months of birth.

An interesting phenomenon is that unlike other diseases this one does not change or grow worse as an individual grows old.

If you have cerebral palsy that affects the arm , only your arms will be affected throughout your lifetime. It does not spread to other body part like cancer does.

OUR LOOKERS

There are over 5 layers in the eyes and each have a unique role.

Your eyes are one of the major parts of the body, they are working from the moment you are awake until the time you close your eyes for bed !!

They take in millions of small pieces of information from the entire world around us - shapes, colors, texture, movement and expressions.

The eye is a round ball that sits in a hollow patch, which is a hole in the skull. The eye lid is present to protect the eye and keep it moist.

The sclera is the white portion of the eyeball. Consider the sclera to be the outer layer of your eyeball.

The iris is the colorful part of the eyes. It has muscles attached which allow change in shape and can adjust the amount of light that can passes through.

The sclera has blood vessels, which are small tubes that transport blood.

The pupil is in the center of the iris. The pupil is a tiny hole, an opening allowing light to pass through it.

In the anterior chamber there is a special fluid present that allows your eye to stay healthy.

The next part is the lenses that reflects the light to the back of the eye.

The retina is located back of your eye. It converts the light into nerve impulses for the brain.

The lenses are held in place by fibers which extend out into attaching the ciliary muscle.

The optic nerve takes all the information from the retina and sends it to the brain.

The muscles help the lens change shape.

Messages travel at lighting fast speed.

HAIR CYCLE

Your hair has a cycle that it follows - it will be born and it will die.

A human has about 100,000 strands of hair.

Because each person's scalp has 100,000 or more hair follicles, the loss of 10 or more hair strands every day doesn't create a significant impact or problem .

Hair grows and dies in phases, each strand can stay of your head for two years.

It is normal to lose 15 to 20 strands of hair a day.

ANAGEN

The phase through which the baby hair is still growing and becoming longer. 90% of the hair strands grow in this stage .

CATAGEN

The next stage is the catagen. The hair stops growing at this stage. It usually lasts between 10 to 20 days- the hair grows slowly

TELOGEN

The telogen is the rest stage. At the end of this 3- to 4-month phase, some of your hair falls out. You lose up to 100 hairs a day.

The falling of hair is a natural phenomena and nothing you can do will stop it. But if there a large amount of hair falling everyday, then there is a problem.

Causes of hair loss

Alopecia - falling out of patches of hair from the body

Genes

Stress

Medical Conditions

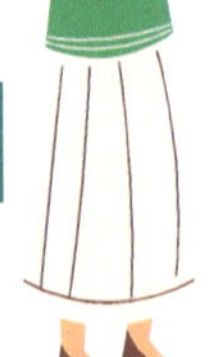

NOSE BLEEDS

Why is it that we have nose bleeds only in the summers?

Dry air is the most common cause for nose bleeding to occur.

When the nose is picked and scratched it also bleeds.

The nasal membrane is irritated by the heat and the hot air. Sometimes the membrane can completely dry up.

Colds harass the inner lines on the nose and this causes continuous sneezing and blowing the nose.

When dust particles enter, they stick to the nasal passages, leading people to pick their nose in response to the discomfort and irritation it causes in breathing.

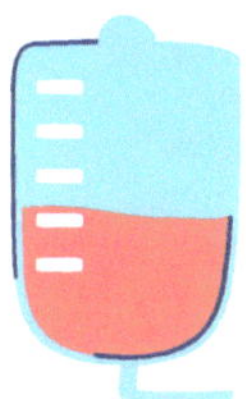

Tiny blood vessels within the nose might become inflamed and fail to repair.

Generally doctors provide medicine to calm down these sensations in the body and also help avoid an individual from reacting to those messages.

If you attempt to stop the bleeding but it continues after 10 minutes, it is important to seek medical attention to avoid excessive blood loss.

The worst that could come out of a nosebleed is a sinus infection or damage to a blood vessel.

Most common type of nosebleeds is the anterior nosebleed. The blood generates from the front of your nose because the blood vessels burst.

Another type of bleeding is known as posterior bleeding where the blood generates from the deepest part of the nose.

THE BONES

If the bones are the innermost part of the body, what makes up the bones.

Did you know that you have 206 bones in total? Bones are used to give your body shape.

LAYERS -
1. Bone marrow - creates cells for the body.
2. Cancellous - guards the bone marrow
3. Cortical - the actual hard bone
4. Periosteum - thin layer that has nerves.

Bones are alive and pumping with life - they are white, young, fresh, and are made up of various materials.

Different parts of the body will have different types of bones.

SPINE

our spine gives us the ability to bend, twist and stand up straight.

CERVICAL - below the brain, supports the back and neck.

THORACIC- They help to hold the ribs in place.

LUMBAR - consists of 5 bones which hold the body weight.

COCCYX - base of the spine and helps in balance, stability.

The bones of the spine are used to protect a spinal cord which is really just a bunch of neurons and nerves bundled together. These bones are known as vertebrae and each of them is shaped like a ring.

Between the vertebrae there are strips of cartilage present which prevent the vertebrae from banging each other.

RIB CAGE

These set of bones secure the heart, lung and the liver.

All 12 pairs of ribs join to the spine in the back, where the thoracic vertebrae keep them in place.

They make sure no harm comes to them to the most important organs of the human body.

THE SKULL

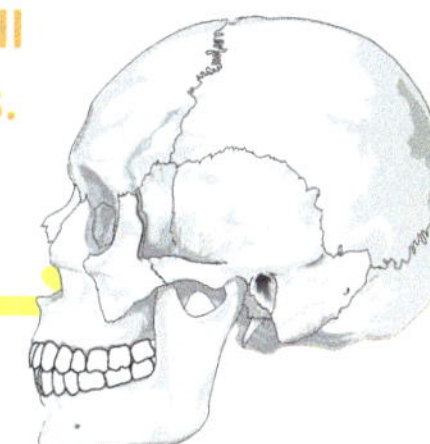

The skull covers your entire face and protects all the interval passage ways.

It has holes for your eyes to be placed and another for the mouth.

The skull protects the most important part of the human body known are the brain.

The smallest bone in the body is present in the head. It is the eardrum.

THE HANDS

You need hands for everything from tying your shoelaces to writing an exam.

Each arm in your body in attached to a scapula which is known are shoulder blade. This blade is triangular and located at the back of the spine.

THE LEGS

FEMUR

The femur is the bone that goes all the way from the pelvis to the knee.

FIBULA

The tibia's main function is to bear weight of the human body. It is the second largest bone.

The pelvis is a circular muscle and is a bowl - shaped that supports the spine. The front of the pelvis is made up of the two major hip bones.

When two bones meet it is known as the joint.

Your joints have their own unique fluid, called synovial fluid, which allows them to move freely.

Ligaments, which act like incredibly strong rubber bands, hold bones together at the joints.

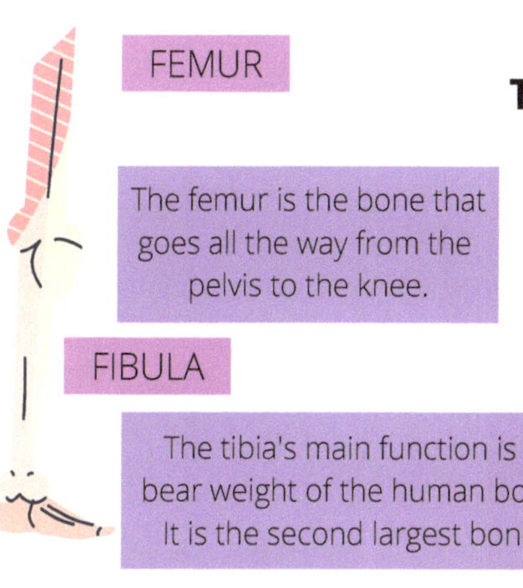

The disease that is uncontrollable and scientists cannot find a solution.

Every human primarily has two lungs which they use to breathe. We have one lung on each side of the body.

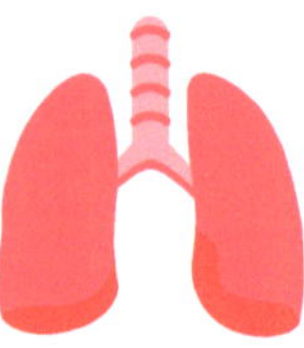

Each lung is made up of a stretchy material and just like a balloon fills up with air.

There are smaller structures that help the lungs in their function. The use of the lungs is for the gaseous exchange where oxygen is absorbed and carbon dioxide is released.

Inside the lungs there are miniature sacs called alveoli. These sacs are the most important part of the breathing and respiration process.

To keep us alive a gas called oxygen is needed. We need oxygen to transport from the air into our blood and another gas called carbon dioxide to move out from the blood and into the air. The carbon dioxide is removed because it is toxic.

Blood runs along the sides of the small bags at the same time. This closes the gap between the air and the blood, allowing the gases to flow in the proper direction.

A sigh is a deeper breath than the ones we usually take and it fills lots of air into the lungs.

If you sigh, any little bags (called alveoli) that aren't being used are filled with air. This prevents them from falling and saves them from harm!

Your brain takes care of breathing for you most of the time, and thankfully, it also takes care of sighing. This means you don't have to be concerned about forgetting to sigh.

NAIL SURVIVAL

Nails might not seem every important but without them we could die.

Humans evolved to have nails because they helped us pick things up and hold onto certain equipment tightly.

Primates first had claws but then they evolved into nails.

Humans are part of the primate family, this family consists of monkeys who were considered the most intelligent mammals at that time. We got our nails from these primates.

When comparing your nails to a cat's claws, you'll observe that your nails are wider, flat, and shield-shaped, while the cat's claws are located at the tips of their fingers and attached to the upper side.

The nails we possess help us well in performing daily activities such as washing dishes, preparing food, picking up objects, and even plucking flowers. However, one may wonder if a claw would be capable of accomplishing these same tasks.

Claws do not allow animals to perform the simple actions that we do everyday.

While claws hold little use for humans, they serve as a significant advantage for cats, enabling them to fulfill various purposes. However, for human needs, claws are simply impractical.

Imagine if humans did not have nails, then what would happen ?

You would find it very hard to do many daily activities because of that soft skin present there. You would not be able to pick things up, put things down - you would not have the ability to drink water with a glass or even eat meals without resorting to cannibalism.

Scientists say that we can even die without nails.

THE COVID 19

Learn about the virus the shut the entire world for 2 years.

A pandemic is a disease the spread from country to country.

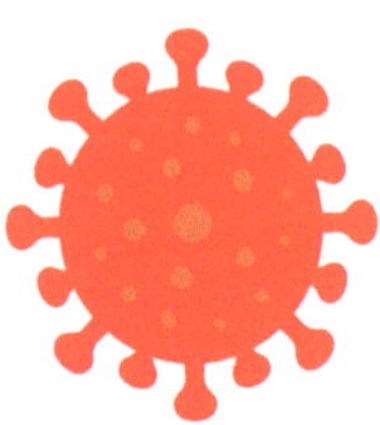

At the end of 2019, a new virus - SARS-CoV-2 also known as Corona Virus emerged from China and spread all around the world.

The Covid 19 can spread very easily, thus surges occur during large gatherings or when people are not wearing masks.

The virus is always evolving and becomes more dangerous and contagious.

If you have Covid you will show a few symptoms which include fever, coughing, breathing trouble and diarrhea.

Some people are more susceptible to the infection. Some people, on the other hand, have no symptoms at all.

Even if they have no symptoms, people can contract COVID-19 from someone who does. When an infected individual breathes, talks, sneezes, or coughs, tiny droplets are released into the air.

These could land in someone's nose, mouth, or eyes, or they can be inhaled in. Air currents carry even the smallest drops, which can stay in the air for minutes to several hours.

Clean things that get touched a lot (like doorknobs, counters, phones, etc.).

Hands should be washed frequently. Wash for at least 20 seconds with soap and water or with a hand sanitizer.

Using masks is still an important part of preventing the spread of the disease. On public transportation, everyone above the age of two should wear a mask.

THE NEW MAN

The skull of a new species of human was found in China.

A perfectly preserved skull of a man was found in Harbin, north - east China.

The scientific name for the Dragon Man is called 'Homo longi' where longi means dragon in chinese.

The skull was said to belong to an ancient man that lived in East Asia at least 146,000 years ago called the 'Dragon Man'.

This new finding can change the course of the entire evolutionary history we currently follow.

The dragon man's brain size much larger than average human's. Other special features of the Dragon Man include square eye sockets, thick brow ridges, a wide mouth, and oversized teeth.

the 'Dragon man' lived in a forested floodplain environment as part of a small community, although there is not much evidence on the statement made by him.

The skull was discovered in 1933, by a construction worker who was helping to build a bridge on the Songhua river running through Harbin, in Heilongjiang province.

He smuggled the skull back home and drowned it in a well next to his house, where it was kept for 80 years.

Just as the man was about to die, he told his family about the skull. The family gave the skull to scientists and researchers in exchange for money.

Scientists are debating whether this new species represents primitive homo sapiens(humans), Neanderthals (ancient humans), or a totally different species known as the Denisovans.

FOOD NEURON

Where does your appetite or food preference come from ?

Food preferences are controlled by a specific brain region and targeting neurons in those brain regions could reduce food cravings.

The neuronal activity in the ventral pallidum, a brain region, is linked to food preferences.

The neurons in the ventral pallidum connected to food decisions made by patients when their preferences varied owing to physiological changes.

In order to make smart judgments that are crucial for survival, your brain has to consider multiple possible outcomes or possibilities.

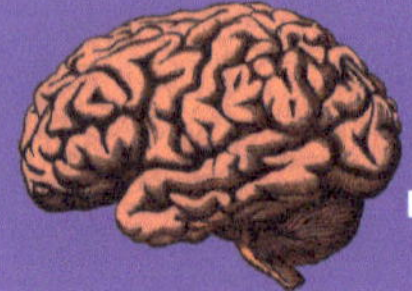

The ventral pallidum is known to play a role in this process. The exact mechanism by which the neurons there accomplish this remained a mystery.

Different neurons responded to plain water, which was favoured while thirsty, and sweetened water, which was preferred when thirst was quenched.

Different neurons respond to favoured food and drink versus what's required to satisfy basic hunger/thirst.

Researchers were also successful in manipulating neurons to make people seek both preferred and undesirable flavours.

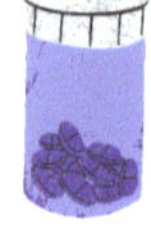

These circuits are comparable to those found in addiction, and they could explain why we prefer drugs to other forms of reward.

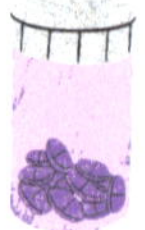

A GOOD CRY

Crying can save your physical health and has multiple benefits.

3 TYPES OF TEARS -

REFLEXIVE TEARS

CONTIINOUS TEARS

EMOTIVE TEARS

Reflex tears remove particles from your eyes, such as smoke and dust.

Emotional tears include stress hormones, continuous tears are 98 percent water.

Crying may be one of your most effective self-soothing techniques.

Crying activates the parasympathetic nervous system. The PNS aids digestion and relaxation for your body.

Crying over lengthy periods of time releases oxytocin and endogenous opioids, also known as endorphins, from the body.

These feel-good molecules can aid in the relief of both physical and mental discomfort.

Your body may fall into a numb state once the endorphins are released. Oxytocin is a hormone that may make you feel calm or happy.

Crying is a good method to let others around you know you need help if you're feeling down.

There is a social benefit to crying

Crying has served as an attachment behavior since infancy, serving the purpose of seeking comfort and care from others. In other words, it contributes to the development of your social support network during challenging times.

WORKS CITED

"A Trick of Nature: Blue Jays Aren't Really Blue." Accelerator, 25 Jan. 2019, www.reconnectwithnature.org/news-events/the-buzz/nature-curiosity-why-are-blue-jays-blue/. Accessed 26 Dec. 2023.

"Bat Echolocation." Dnr.maryland.gov, dnr.maryland.gov/wildlife/Pages/plants_wildlife/bats/batelocu.aspx. Accessed 26 Dec. 2023.

Better Health Channel. "Bones." Vic.gov.au, 31 Oct. 2012, www.betterhealth.vic.gov.au/health/conditionsandtreatments/bones.

---. "Immune System." Vic.gov.au, 2017, www.betterhealth.vic.gov.au/health/conditionsandtreatments/immune-system.

---. "Mouth." Vic.gov.au, 2012, www.betterhealth.vic.gov.au/health/conditionsandtreatments/mouth.

Boyd, Kierstan, and David Turbert. "Parts of the Eye." American Academy of Ophthalmology, 21 Dec. 2018, www.aao.org/eye-health/anatomy/parts-of-eye.

Centers for Disease Control and Prevention. "About COVID-19." Centers for Disease Control and Prevention, 10 July 2023, www.cdc.gov/coronavirus/2019-ncov/your-health/about-covid-19.html.

Fisheries, NOAA. "Why Do Whales Migrate? They Return to the Tropics to Shed Their Skin, Scientists Say | NOAA Fisheries." NOAA, 6 Jan. 2021, www.fisheries.noaa.gov/feature-story/why-do-whales-migrate-they-return-tropics-shed-their-skin-scientists-say.

Flecher, Jenna. "Appetite: What It Is, What Affects It, and How to Change It." Www.medicalnewstoday.com, 14 July 2020, www.medicalnewstoday.com/articles/appetite#summary.

Gillot, Caroline. "Nosebleeds: Causes, Treatment, and Home Remedies." Www.medicalnewstoday.com, 9 Feb. 2023, www.medicalnewstoday.com/articles/164823.

Harding, Lucy. "We Solved the Mystery of Why Some Fish Are Warm-Blooded." The Conversation, 5 June 2021, theconversation.com/we-solved-the-mystery-of-why-some-fish-are-warm-blooded-163774.

"Japanese Snow Monkeys Get Stress Relief, Warmth in Hot Springs." Animals, 4 Apr. 2018, www.nationalgeographic.com/animals/article/japanese-snow-monkey-macaques-bath-stress-spd.

"Life Cycle of Hair." CRLAB EN, 29 June 2021, crlab.com/en_en/scientific-area/hair-and-scalp/life-cycle-of-hair/. Accessed 26 Dec. 2023.

Magazine, Smithsonian, and Shi En Kim. "Fourteen Ways That Spiders Use Their Silk." Smithsonian Magazine, 27 Oct. 2021, www.smithsonianmag.com/science-nature/fourteen-ways-spiders-use-their-silk-180978354/#:~:text=Spider%20silk%20is%20a%20wonder.

published, Bahar Gholipour. "Why Do Babies Barely Blink?" Livescience.com, 5 July 2018, www.livescience.com/62988-why-babies-rarely-blink.html.

SeaWorld Parks & Entertainment. "All about Killer Whales - Communication & Echolocation | SeaWorld Parks & Entertainment." Seaworld.org, 2019, seaworld.org/animals/all-about/killer-whale/communication/.

Stanford Children's Health. "Anatomy and Physiology of the Ear." Stanfordchildrens.org, 2019, www.stanfordchildrens.org/en/topic/default?id=anatomy-and-physiology-of-the-ear-90-P02025.

Harris, Rob. "How Does the Squid's Eye Help It Survive in Its Environment?" Pets on Mom.com, animals.mom.com/squids-eye-survive-its-environment-8618.html.

Hines, Tonya. "Anatomy of the Human Brain." Mayfield Clinic, Apr. 2018, mayfieldclinic.com/pe-anatbrain.htm.

"How Noise Pollution May Harm the Heart." Harvard Health, 1 Mar. 2020, www.health.harvard.edu/heart-health/how-noise-pollution-may-harm-the-heart.

Jha, Alok. "Toads Able to Detect Earthquake Days Beforehand, Says Study." The Guardian, 31 Mar. 2010, www.theguardian.com/science/2010/mar/31/toads-detect-earthquakes-study.

Johnston, Hamish . "Why Peregrine Falcons Wear Eyeliner, Golden Eagles Could Accelerate Using Turbulence." Physics World, 4 June 2021, physicsworld.com/a/why-peregrine-falcons-wear-eyeliner-golden-eagles-could-accelerate-using-turbulence/.

Jones, Alexander. "Understanding the Mechanisms behind Lyme Disease." Futurum Careers, 2021, https://doi.org/10.33424/futurum142. Accessed 2 June 2021.

Khanna, Monit. "Climate Change: Dragonfly Are Losing Their Shine and May Slowly Be Lost Forever." IndiaTimes, 7 July 2021, www.indiatimes.com/technology/science-and-future/climate-change-dragonfly-shine-loss-544430.html. Accessed 26 Dec. 2023.

Magazine, Hakai. "The Secret of This Puffin's Big Beak." Hakai Magazine, 16 Jan. 2020, hakaimagazine.com/news/the-secret-of-this-puffins-big-beak/.

Marcin, Ashley. "9 Ways Crying May Benefit Your Health." Healthline, Healthline Media, 14 Apr. 2017, www.healthline.com/health/benefits-of-crying.

Maryland, University of. "Mice Were Kept in the Dark for One Week – Their Brain Cell Networks Rewired and Hearing Sensitivity Changed." SciTechDaily, 4 Dec. 2019, scitechdaily.com/mice-were-kept-in-the-dark-for-one-week-their-brain-cell-networks-rewired-and-hearing-sensitivity-changed/. Accessed 26 Dec. 2023.

McSpadden, Kevin. "You Now Have a Shorter Attention Span than a Goldfish." Time, 14 May 2015, time.com/3858309/attention-spans-goldfish/.

National Institute on Aging. "Parkinson's Disease." National Institute on Aging, 14 Apr. 2022, www.nia.nih.gov/health/parkinsons-disease#:~:text=Parkinson.

Nordqvist, Joseph. "Brain Freeze: The Science behind Ice Cream Headache." Www.medicalnewstoday.com, 30 Mar. 2017, www.medicalnewstoday.com/articles/244458.

Pollock, Jessica. "Why Don't Hummingbirds Get Fat or Sick from Drinking Sugary Nectar?" The Conversation, 23 Aug. 2019, theconversation.com/why-dont-hummingbirds-get-fat-or-sick-from-drinking-sugary-nectar-122178. Accessed 26 Dec. 2023.

Prasher, Shantanu . "This Is the Reason Why That One Friend of Yours Eats Everything but Never Gets Fat." Www.mensxp.com, 9 Dec. 2017, www.mensxp.com/health/nutrition/41218-this-is-the-reason-why-that-one-friend-of-yours-who-eats-everything-but-never-gets-fat.html. Accessed 26 Dec. 2023.

Rasmussen, Cindy . "Crocodile Eyes: What Makes Them so Unique?" AZ Animals, 23 Mar. 2022, a-z-animals.com/blog/crocodile-eyes-what-makes-them-so-unique/.

Summers, Becky. "Why Do Our Fingers and Toes Wrinkle during a Bath?" Scientific American, 9 Jan. 2013, www.scientificamerican.com/article/why-do-our-fingers-and-toes-wrinkle-during-a-bath/.

Community, The NCF. "Bird Migrations : Adaptations and Threats." Nature Conservation Foundation - India, 31 Oct. 2021, www.ncf-india.org/blog/bird-migrations-adaptations-and-threats.

Jancikin, Olivera . "How Long Does a Snail Sleep? Can They Do It for 3 Years? - Sleep Advisor." Sleep Advisor, 8 Oct. 2021, www.sleepadvisor.org/how-long-do-snails-sleep/.

Melinda. "Sleep Needs - HelpGuide.org." Https://Www.helpguide.org, 2 Nov. 2018, www.helpguide.org/articles/sleep/sleep-needs-get-the-sleep-you-need.htm.

Nall, Rachel . "Why Do We Have Nails? The Important Roles They Play." Healthline, 22 Apr. 2020, www.healthline.com/health/why-do-we-have-nails#:~:text=The%20fingernails%20have%20many%20small.

Raypole, Crystal. "Yes, Blind People Dream, Too." Healthline, Healthline Media, 5 Aug. 2019, www.healthline.com/health/can-blind-people-dream.

Sargen, Molly . "Biological Roles of Water: Why Is Water Necessary for Life?" Science in the News, 26 Sept. 2019, sitn.hms.harvard.edu/uncategorized/2019/biological-roles-of-water-why-is-water-necessary-for-life/.

Scarton, Dana. "The Importance of the Pinkie, Experienced Firsthand." The New York Times, 16 Dec. 2008, www.nytimes.com/2008/12/18/health/18iht-snpinkie.1.18718834.html.

"Sickle Cell Anemia - Symptoms and Causes." Mayo Clinic, 2018, www.mayoclinic.org/diseases-conditions/sickle-cell-anemia/symptoms-causes/syc-20355876.

Sivadas, Athira. "Digital Object Identifier System." Doi.org, 2018, doi.org.
Staff, A. G. "Friend or Foe: How Bottlenose Dolphins Keep Track of Their Social Alliances." Australian Geographic, 8 June 2018, www.australiangeographic.com.au/topics/wildlife/2018/06/friend-or-foe-how-bottlenose-dolphins-keep-track-of-their-social-alliances/. Accessed 26 Dec. 2023.

Stierwalt, Everyday Einstein Sabrina. "Can Science Explain Deja Vu?" Scientific American, www.scientificamerican.com/article/can-science-explain-deja-vu/. Accessed 26 Dec. 2023.

"The Science of Tanning: Understand the True Impact on Your Skin." LifeJacket Skin Protection, 17 May 2023, lifejacketskin.com/blogs/lifejournal/science-of-tanning. Accessed 26 Dec. 2023.

"Why Do We Have Nails? Let's Find out Its Role in Keeping Us Healthy." Onlymyhealth, 20 Sept. 2021, www.onlymyhealth.com/why-do-we-have-nails-explains-expert-1631713476.

Cleveland Clinic. "Metabolism: What It Is, How It Works and Disorders." Cleveland Clinic, 30 Aug. 2021, my.clevelandclinic.org/health/body/21893-metabolism.

Exeter, University of. "Otters Juggle Stones – Now Researchers Think They Know Why [Video]." SciTechDaily, 7 May 2020, scitechdaily.com/otters-juggle-stones-now-researchers-think-they-know-why-video/.

Team, Ben. "How Often Do Rattlesnakes Sleep?" Pets on Mom.com, animals.mom.com/rattlesnakes-sleep-10795.html. Accessed 26 Dec. 2023.

CDC. "What Is Cerebral Palsy? | CDC." Centers for Disease Control and Prevention, 2 Sept. 2021, www.cdc.gov/ncbddd/cp/facts.html#:~:text=CP%20is%20the%20most%20common.

"Human Teeth Are as Strong as a Shark's Teeth." Independent.ie, 1 Aug. 2012, www.independent.ie/life/health-wellbeing/human-teeth-are-as-strong-as-a-sharks-teeth/26882223.html.

"Locomotion in the Ocean: How Sea Animals Move." Two Oceans Aquarium, 17 July 2020, www.aquarium.co.za/news/locomotion-in-the-ocean-how-sea-animals-move-part-2.

Tikaken, Amy. "Why Do Horses Sleep Standing Up?" Encyclopedia Britannica, www.britannica.com/story/why-do-horses-sleep-standing-up#:~:text=To%20protect%20themselves%2C%20horses%20instead.

Today, Telangana. "Why Do Tigers Have Whiskers?" Telangana Today, 13 Dec. 2020, telanganatoday.com/why-do-tigers-have-whiskers. Accessed 26 Dec. 2023.

"What Is Sociocultural? - Definition | Meaning | Example." My Accounting Course, 2019, www.myaccountingcourse.com/accounting-dictionary/sociocultural.

"Why Do Bats Sleep Upside Down? | Wonderopolis." Wonderopolis.org, wonderopolis.org/wonder/Why-Do-Bats-Sleep-Upside-Down.

"Why Do Pufferfish "Puff Up"? | Seattle Aquarium." Www.seattleaquarium.org, www.seattleaquarium.org/blog/why-do-pufferfish-puff#:~:text=Pufferfish%20will%20%E2%80%9Cpuff%20up%E2%80%9D%20as.

Zeidan, Adam. "Why Do Mosquito Bites Itch?" Encyclopedia Britannica, www.britannica.com/story/why-do-mosquito-bites-itch.

Zimmer, Carl. "Discovery of "Dragon Man" Skull in China May Add Species to Human Family Tree." The New York Times, 25 June 2021, www.nytimes.com/2021/06/25/science/dragon-man-skull-china.html.

"The Psychology of Intuition (Trusting Your Gut)." Management and Teams, 3 Apr. 2022, www.russellfutcher.com/new-blog/2022/2/14/the-psychology-of-intuition-trusting-your-gut#:~:text=Gut%20feelings%20or%20intuitions%20come.

"Teeth: Types, Function & Care." Cleveland Clinic, 2023, my.clevelandclinic.org/health/body/24655-teeth.

Weybright, Scott, et al. "Fungus Fights Mites That Harm Honey Bees." WSU Insider, 27 May 2021, news.wsu.edu/press-release/2021/05/27/fungus-fights-mites-harm-honey-bees/.